Mount Rushmore

Judith Jango-Cohen

Lerner Publications Company

Minneapolis

To my niece Carla,
who has big dreams
like Gutzon Borglum

-J.J.

Lerner Publications Company
A division of Lerner Publishing Group, Inc.
241 First Avenue North
Minneapolis, MN 55401 U.S.A.

Website address: www.lernerbooks.com

Library of Congress Cataloging-in-Publication Data

Jango-Cohen, Judith.
    Mount Rushmore / by Judith Jango-Cohen.
        p.   cm. — (Lightning bolt books™ — Famous places)
    Includes index.
    ISBN 978-0-7613-6021-6 (lib. bdg. : alk. paper)
    1. Mount Rushmore National Memorial (S.D.)—Juvenile literature. I. Title.
    F657.R8J366 2011
    978.3'93—dc22   2009038847

Manufactured in the United States of America
1 — BP — 7/15/10

Contents

Famous Faces

Whose giant face is this?

It's the face of President George Washington. His face is carved into Mount Rushmore in South Dakota.

George Washington is known as the father of our country.

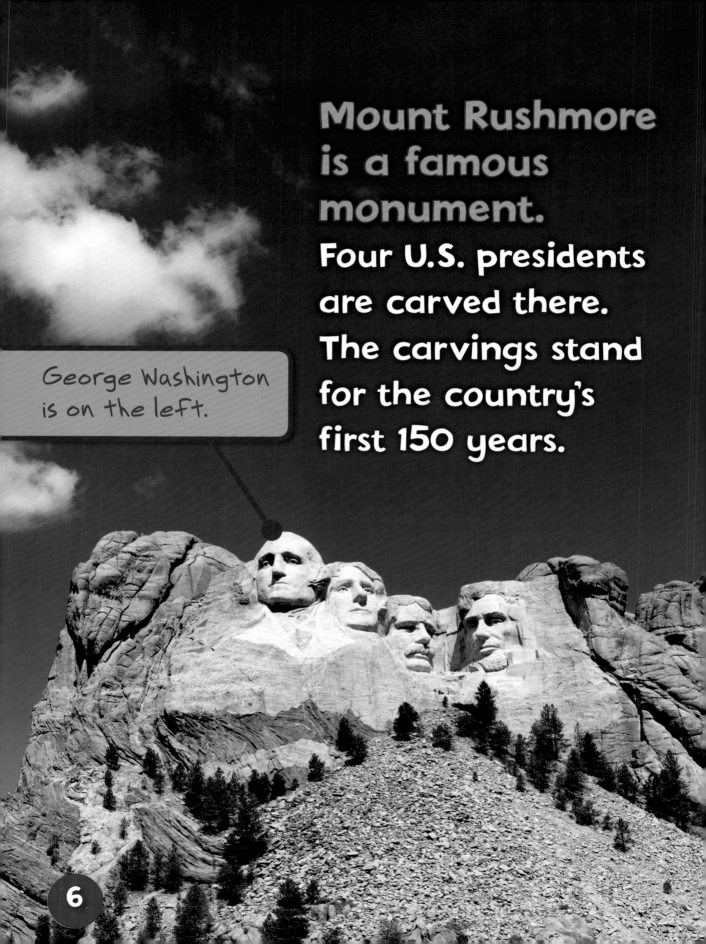

Mount Rushmore is a famous monument. Four U.S. presidents are carved there. The carvings stand for the country's first 150 years.

George Washington is on the left.

Planning Mount Rushmore

Gutzon Borglum had the idea to make Mount Rushmore. Many people in South Dakota liked his idea.

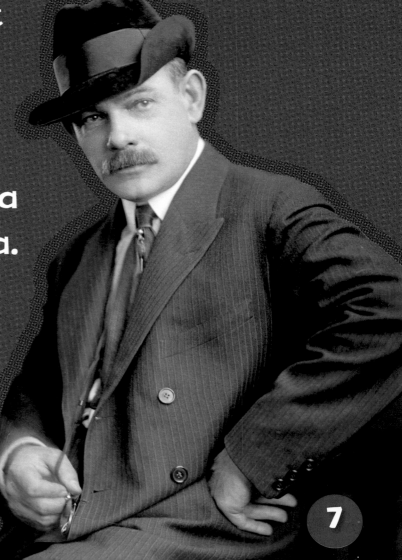

So Gutzon looked for a tall, sunny mountain for his carving. His son Lincoln helped him. In 1925, they chose Mount Rushmore.

This is what Mount Rushmore looked like before Gutzon carved it.

Gutzon decided to carve Washington. He was the first U.S. president. Why did Gutzon choose the others?

Thomas Jefferson added new land to the United States. This land made the country twice as big.

Thomas Jefferson was the third president of the United States.

Abraham Lincoln led the United States during the Civil War (1861–1865). The North and South fought each other. But Lincoln kept the country together.

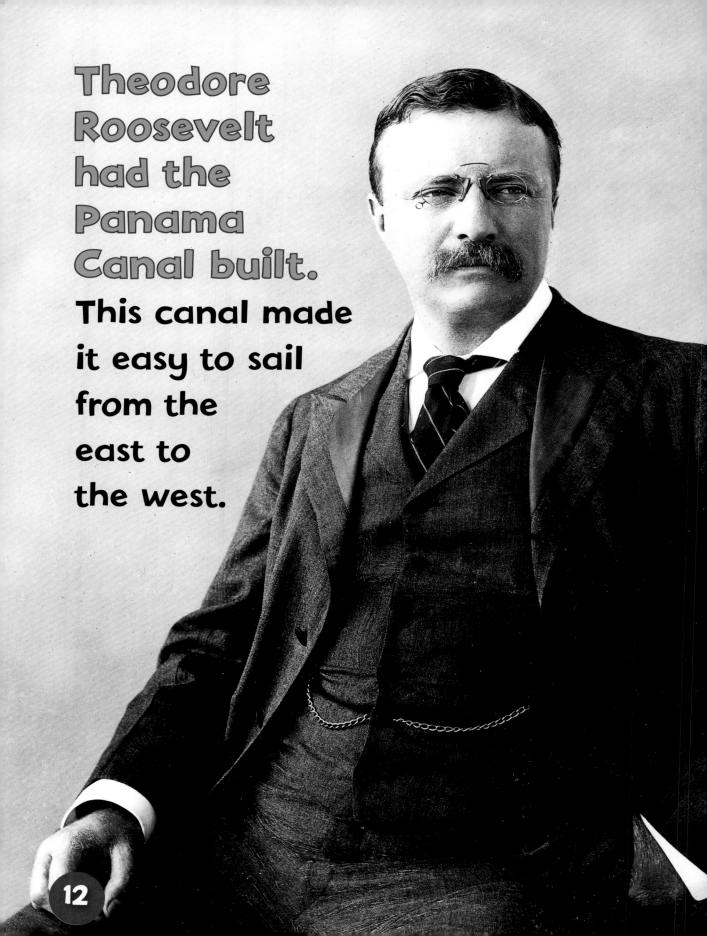

Theodore Roosevelt had the Panama Canal built. This canal made it easy to sail from the east to the west.

Making Mount Rushmore

Gutzon made a model of the presidents. The model helped his workers make the giant carving.

Gutzon's model was much smaller than the actual carving would be.

In 1927, the carving of Mount Rushmore began. How do you think workers broke away the stone?

Stone carvers work on Mount Rushmore.

Workers blasted away big blocks of rock with dynamite.
The mountain rumbled with each dynamite blast.

A dynamite blast knocks rocks off the mountain.

Workers used drills to break away smaller chunks of stone. Drillers worked high up on the mountain. They worked in cages and in seats that looked like swings.

Workers in wooden cages carve George Washington's face.

Steel wires, called cables, held the workers on the mountain.

Steel cables hold this worker high above the ground.

Gutzon watched over the workers. He also made safety rules.

Gutzon watches as workers carve an eye on Mount Rushmore.

Gutzon could not be at Mount Rushmore all the time. His son took over when Gutzon was gone.

Gutzon's son Lincoln Borglum also worked on Mount Rushmore.

Each night, dusty and tired men walked 760 steps down the mountain.

Workers stand on the snow-covered steps that lead to the top of Mount Rushmore.

By 1936, workers rode up and down the mountain in a wooden cage.

This wooden cage carried workers and equipment to the top of the mountain.

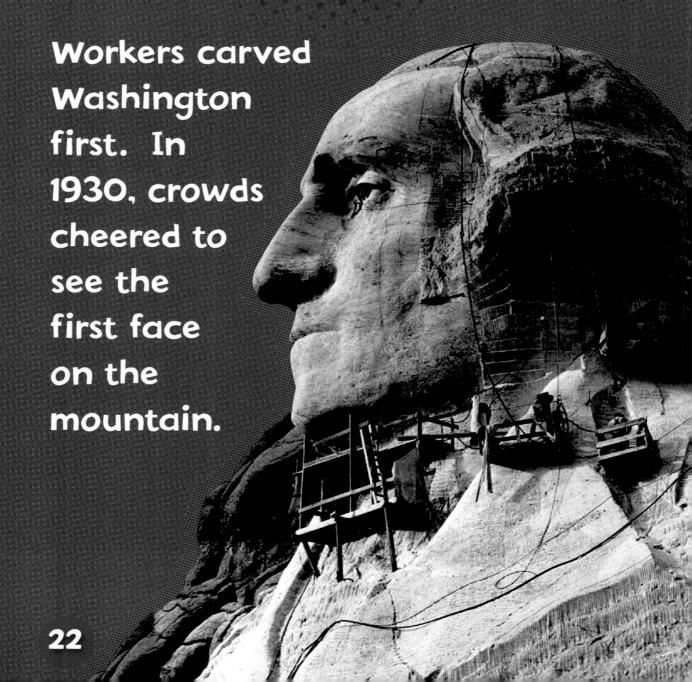

Taking Shape

Workers carved Washington first. In 1930, crowds cheered to see the first face on the mountain.

People came to see the carving of Jefferson in 1936. One year later, they cheered when Lincoln's face appeared.

Stone carvers work on Lincoln's face.

In 1939, Theodore Roosevelt looked out from Mount Rushmore. By 1941, the last bits of work were done.

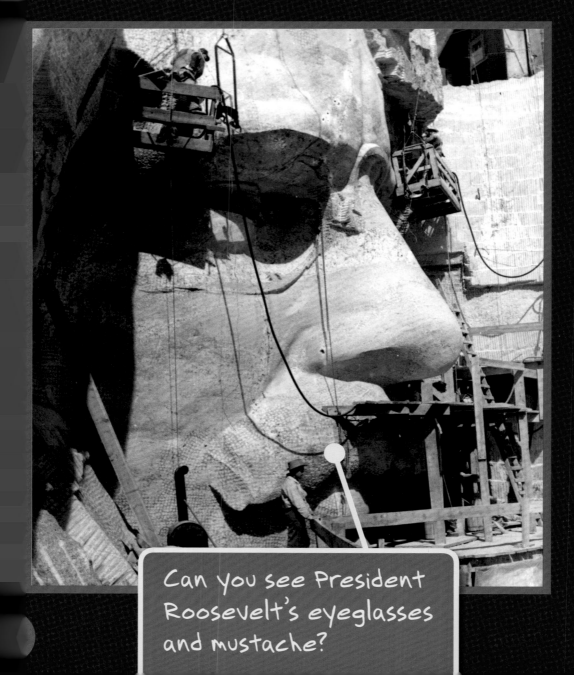

Can you see President Roosevelt's eyeglasses and mustache?

A Lasting Monument

About four hundred people worked on Mount Rushmore. They are listed at the mountain. Their grandchildren come to read their names.

Millions of people visit
Mount Rushmore.
The mountain
is a very
famous site.

Gutzon made the monument
to honor the United States.
He hoped it would last for
years to come.

Mount Rushmore Area

CANADA

MONTANA

NORTH DAKOTA

MINNESOTA

N

SOUTH DAKOTA

WYOMING

Rapid City

Mount Rushmore National Memorial

Missouri River

IOWA

NEBRASKA

Miles

0   25   50   75   100

0   50   100   150

Kilometers

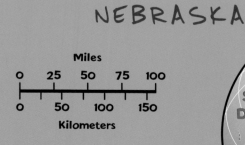

South Dakota

UNITED STATES

Fun Facts

- The faces on Mount Rushmore are 60 feet (18 meters) high. That's about as tall as a five-story building.

- Gutzon wanted to carve Jefferson on the end of the row of presidents. But the stone was not strong there. So Gutzon carved Jefferson on the other side of Washington.

- Some of the drills workers used weighed more than 80 pounds (36 kilograms). That may be more than you weigh!

- Some workers were afraid of hanging over the edge of the mountain in the cages and seats. At home at night, they had bad dreams and woke up hanging onto their beds. Gutzon gave these workers other jobs.

- Gutzon died on March 6, 1941, before his carving was done. His son Lincoln took over for him until the work was finished on October 31, 1941.

Glossary

cable: a strong wire made of twisted steel

canal: a waterway or path dug for water to flow through and boats to sail across

Civil War: a war between two groups of people in one country. In the 1860s, the people living in the North of the United States fought those living in the South.

drill: a tool with a pointed end that can cut into stone and other hard things

dynamite: a special powder or material that can blow apart stone and other hard, strong things

model: a small copy of something

monument: a statue, building, or other structure that is made to remember a person or event

president: the leader of a country, such as the United States

Further Reading

American Experience: Mount Rushmore
http://www.pbs.org/wgbh/amex/rushmore

Enchanted Learning: Mount Rushmore
http://www.enchantedlearning.com/
history/us/monuments/mtrushmore

Kishel, Ann-Marie. *Thomas Jefferson:
A Life of Patriotism.* Minneapolis:
Lerner Publications Company, 2006.

Mara, Wil. *Theodore Roosevelt.*
New York: Children's Press, 2007.

National Park
Service: Mount
Rushmore National
Memorial
http://www.nps.gov/
moru/index.htm

Nelson, Robin. *George Washington: A Life of
Leadership.* Minneapolis: Lerner Publications
Company, 2006.

Index

Photo Acknowledgments

The images in this book are used with the permission of: © Darren Green/Dreamstime. com, p. 4; © Victoria Short/Dreamstime.com, p. 5; © Ron Chapple Studios/Dreamstime. com, pp. 6, 30; Library of Congress, pp. 7 (LC-DIG-hec-19092), 11 (LC-DIG-ppmsca-19215), 12 (LC-USZ62-106668), 13 (LC-USZ62-105079); CSU Archv/Everett/Rex Features USA, p. 8; © Museum of the City of New York/CORBIS, p. 9; Independence National Historical Park, p. 10; © Underwood & Underwood/CORBIS, pp. 14, 18, 21; Lincoln Borglum, p. 15; © Alfred Eisenstaedt/Pix Inc./Time & Life Pictures/Getty Images, p. 16; AP Photo, pp. 17, 19, 22, 24, 31; Bell Photo, p. 20; © Frederic Lewis/Hulton Archive/ Getty Images, p. 23; © Judith Jango-Cohen, p. 25; © Jonathan Larsen/Diadem Images/Alamy, pp. 26–27; © Laura Westlund/Independent Picture Service, p. 28.

Cover: © Olivier Le Queinec/Dreamstime.com.